CW00550189

The Throws and Take-downs of

Judo

Geoff Thompson

SUMMERSDALE

Copyright © Geoff Thompson 2001

All rights reserved. The right of Geoff Thompson to be identified as the author of this work has been asserted in accordance with the Copyright, Designs and Patents Act of 1988.

No part of this book may be reproduced by any means, nor translated into a machine language, without the written permission of the publisher.

Summersdale Publishers Ltd
46 West Street
Chichester
West Sussex
PO19 1RP
United Kingdom

www.summersdale.com

Printed and bound in Great Britain.

ISBN 1 84024 026 1

First edit by Kerry Thompson.

Photographs by David W. Monks, member of the Master Photographers' Association
Snappy Snaps Portrait Studio
7 Cross Cheaping
Coventry
CV1 1HF

Important note

If you have or believe you may have a medical condition the techniques outlined in this book should not be attempted without first consulting your doctor. Some of the techniques in this book require a high level of fitness and suppleness and should not be attempted by someone lacking such fitness. The author and the publishers cannot accept any responsibility for any proceedings or prosecutions brought or instituted against any person or body as a result of the use or misuse of any techniques described in this book or any loss, injury or damage caused thereby.

About the author

Geoff Thompson has written over 20 books and is known worldwide for his bestselling autobiography, *Watch My Back*, about his nine years working as a nightclub doorman. He currently has a quarter of a million books in print. He holds the rank of 6th Dan black belt in Japanese karate, 1st Dan in judo and is also qualified to senior instructor level in various other forms of wrestling and martial arts. He has several scripts for stage and screen in development with Destiny Films.

He has published articles for *GQ* magazine, and has also been featured in *FHM*, *Maxim*, *Arena*, *Front* and *Loaded* magazines, and has appeared many times on mainstream television. Geoff is currently a contributing editor for *Men's Fitness* magazine.

Geoff was trained in judo by British judo champion Wayne Lakin and Olympic silver medallist Neil Adams OBE; he spent 18 months as a full-time judo student in Neil Adams' international class in Coventry, England. He qualified as a black belt with the BJA under the legendary judoka Alan Petherbridge 9th **Dan OBE.**

Thank you to Wayne Lakin for years of private tuition and friendship, also to Neil Adams for allowing me into his elite full-time class. Thank you to all the lads at Neil's for looking after me and for being patient. Also to the legendary Alan Petherbridge OBE for taking me under his wing.

For a free colour brochure of Geoff Thompson's
books and videos please ring the
24-hour hotline on 02476 431100 or write to:

Geoff Thompson Ltd
PO Box 307
Coventry
CV3 2YP

www.geoffthompson.com
www.summersdale.com

Contents

Judo

Introduction

There has been a lot said of late about the art of grappling or, more specifically, the art of ground fighting. The grappling arts are enjoying a well-earned and long-awaited revival. Grappling was in vogue in the early part of this century, a period known as the Golden Age of Wrestling, but it popularity waned just before – and probably due to – the Great War, only to be reborn post-war as 'show grappling'.

It would seem that grappling has always lain hidden within the shadow of contemporary combat, probably due to its unembellished demeanour. Its devastating potency is often hidden (to the uninitiated) by its lack of obvious aesthetic; people have been drawn instead to the superfluously spectacular kicking arts. However, the world of combat, and more specifically the world of martial arts, has now evolved and many of the more spectacular systems have failed the acid test of time and the pressure test of reality. They have crumbled under the weight of contemporary violence like a paper house in a hurricane. The prettier systems that originally drew thousands like summer moths to a flame have balked at the obstacle of practicality, proving to be little more than showy glitz. The fundamental movements of the grappling arts, so often ignored due to the 'ugly duckling' syndrome, have risen above the maelstrom; the swan of real combat has blossomed leaving the 'flash' dead in the water.

Due to the well-publicised rise of the UFC (Ultimate Fight Competition) – cage fighting, reality combat and extreme fighting, everybody suddenly wants to fight on the floor, often to the detriment of all other ranges. I can understand this, ground grappling has been missing from martial arts for so long, and the UFC-type tournaments advertise grappling supremacy so well, it is only natural that people want to fill their baskets with the 'missing range'. Suddenly everyone (and his dog) is desperate to make up for their lack and learn the art of ground fighting. And so they should. I've been trying to tell people this for the last ten years. Having worked as a nightclub doorman for nine years I always knew that grappling was a vital part of the martial armoury. But this is where the

Judo

problems begin. Whilst it is important, even imperative to include grappling on the curriculum it should not be to the exclusion of the other ranges. Martial artists are abandoning their base style to become grapplers. This will do little more than move their weak link from one section of the martial chain to another. They become very good at the match-fight scenario where grapplers rule supreme, but wholly inadequate when it comes to anything involving the other ranges.

My speciality is adapting combat techniques to the street scenario, making it work outside the chip shop and for street-defence, specifically 3-second fighting and ambush fighting. Grappling can be very weak in this arena due to the four B's: biting, butting, blinding and buddies. You have to know grappling of course; you need a map around all of the combat ranges even if it is only to enable you to avoid the traps, but don't make this one range – or any range for that matter – your be all and end all. I have become a good grappler so that I can anti-grapple, and in a worst-case scenario so that I can escape from a bad position on the floor should I make a mistake and find myself there. The fighter who becomes a great grappler because he has watched the reality tapes can find himself getting punched out in the bar by a 3-second fighter, or kicked to death by a football fan with not a single day of formal martial arts to his name. So let's keep things in context. Grapple, yes; but never neglect the other ranges that make up the armoury. If one range is neglected then you have a chink in the armour; you may be judged in a real situation on the strength of that one range, as they say, you are only as strong as your weakest link.

Equally with the ground-fighting phenomenon there has been little or no notice taken of the tachi waza, or standing techniques. A lot of what happens on the floor (unless you are an exceptional ground fighter) is wholly determined by how you got there. If you are thrown, dragged, kicked or punched to the floor and end up in a bad position you may never escape, or your opponent may be in a position to stand back up and kick pieces off you while you are on your back.

Judo

When we practise ground fighting we start from a neutral position. Both fighters with an equal start. In a real situation there is no such neutrality and you very much have to make the best of what you are given, that is unless you are the one who controls the take-down. The question that I always ask when watching demos of ground fighting prowess is, 'Yeah, but how do you get to that position from vertical fighting?' Thus my quest to learn the throws and take-downs from as many systems as possible began.

In this volume we will look specifically at the basic throws and take-downs of judo. Having studied this system for quite a chunk of my life I can vouch for the potency and dynamism of this much-underrated art.

As with ground fighting, don't make the throws and take-downs the be all and end all. Many opponents in a live scenario will not allow you to throw them cleanly, they will grip you like their very lives depend upon it and drag you to the floor with them and if you don't know how to fight on the floor then you are up the proverbial creek.

As I have said in all of the books and videos that I put out, please don't rely on this book, or any other for that matter, to teach you, it must be used in combination with a good class or a good training partner. There is nothing like a real opponent to perfect the physical technique; I'd go as far as to say that it cannot be learned properly by book alone. Learn the fundamentals of the technique, and then put it under the pressure of a non-compliant partner to perfect it. Once you can work the technique on someone that doesn't want to be thrown, then you know you've got it off.

Compliance kills!

Compliance in training is only of use when first learning the fundamentals of a technique; once learned, an opponent should offer 100 per cent resistance. Taking the randori (free-fighting or sparring) out of a system is effectively taking the

Judo

teeth out of it. If there is no adversity, as they say, there is no advance.

Good luck with the practise and thank you for taking the time to read this book.

Chapter One
Balance, Stance, Grip

Let's start with the base. In the journey of a hundred miles the base is the first step. Knowing all the throws in the world won't help if you haven't got your balance or stance right. It is hard to throw an opponent (and easy to be thrown) when the balance is off. And to be brutally honest with you, balance will only come from having a pull on the mat with another player. What I can give you here is the fundamentals so that you can practise correctly from the very beginning. Hopefully this book will act as an appetiser for you to actually start a grappling class or even take private lessons from a local black belt.

The basic grappling stance is similar to the basic karate stance, only a lot smaller.

Presuming that you are working from a left lead (this of course can be reversed) you should stand in a small 45-degree stance.

Judo

The lead leg should be slightly bent at the knees and relaxed. The 45-degree stance allows you the right balance to throw an opponent and to stop him from throwing you. All the time that you move around, gripping the opponent and him gripping you, it is important to maintain this stance or you will be thrown. The only time the stance should change is when you enter to take a throw. If your throw is successful, or even if it is not, you should immediately revert back to the stance. If you do successfully throw the opponent you have the option of following him to the floor for ne-waza (ground fighting) or staying on your feet.

From this stance the left (lead) hand should reach to grip the opponent's right lapel (or shirt, coat, neck or hair if the situation was a street encounter). The right hand grips the opponent's left sleeve or wrist, or in the case of wrestling perhaps around the back of the triceps (upper arm).

This is the basic stance and grip to take when looking for a throw. In a street scenario you may not have the luxury to choose a grip, you may have to take what is given. It doesn't matter much because once all the throws have been mastered you'll be able to take an opponent over from any grip and from any position. For now though we have to be content to work with the fundamentals until such time as we are more competent with the grips and throws.

The grips being described in this book are nothing more than basic and, depending upon how far you wish to take the art of grappling, whole books are available which are filled with different ways to dominate the grip of an opponent. At a high-level competition it is usually the better grip fighter who dominates and thus wins the day. Excellence in grip work also allows small players to completely dominate large players with lesser gripping ability. If you want more information on this subject I would refer you to the excellent book on grips by my friend Neil Adams, one of the best grip fighters on the planet at this moment in time.

So for now we should be content with basic grips, not forgetting the fact that we are very unlikely to meet any trained grapplers in a street attack (we hope). For the street, where fine motor actions are redundant when the adrenal syndrome is triggered, basic is what works best because it generally involves gross motor skills (big, simple movements). These are less affected by the presence of stress.

Once we have the basic stance and grip we use them to break the balance of our opponent. On the street we are unlikely to encounter anyone with great balance though they may have an innate ability to stay vertical, so they will not always be easy to move. On a dojo level however you will be working with players who do have great balance and it becomes a game of breaking balance as a precursor to the throw. In fact with a player of equal skill you are very unlikely to throw them at all without breaking balance first. This is slightly out of the context of this book as we are more concerned here with the attacker on the street than we are with the player in the dojo.

Judo

Basically we break the balance of an opponent with pulling or pushing actions, or by feigning one throw to unbalance him, thus leaving him vulnerable for the second throw.

You break the opponent's balance by pushing or pulling him to the left rear, directly behind, to the right rear or directly to his right or left. Alternatively you can pull the opponent directly towards you, to your left rear or right rear or directly to the right or left. You can also pull him downward.

Any one of these actions will force the opponent to move, hopefully out of stance and off balance, and when he does you can execute a throw.

The other time to take an opponent off balance and take the throw is when he attempts his attack (a throw or punch for example) and you take advantage of his stance change to take him over. This is something that has to be felt and cannot be properly related via the pages of a book.

Stiff Arming

There is a term that is recognised in most forms of grappling

called 'stiff arming'.

Judo

Stiff arming usually occurs with less skilful opponents, especially the type that you will meet in a street encounter, who literally hold you to the spot with their strength normally out of sheer terror of being thrown. They do not attack or defend, they just hold – very tightly. Dealing with stiff armers requires good grip work and a good sense of flow, using their strength against them by going with the flow of energy. If it's a street encounter you can kick them (anywhere) or strike them with any available technique before you attempt a throw. It goes without saying that in most grappling sports this would be frowned upon so don't do it, or if you do don't tell them that I said you could! The blow before the throw will break the balance of the stiff armer, creating a window of opportunity; *then* you bang in the throw.

If you encounter a fighter with no or little clothing to grab then the throwing technique has to change slightly. You need to revert to the wrestling type grips and use the opponent's limbs to grip as opposed to the clothing. From my experience of working with several systems of grappling the wrestling take-downs are favourite here because they do not rely upon clothing to take an opponent over. Some of the Greco (Greco-Roman wrestling) snatches and freestyle leg take-downs come into their own in this scenario.

It is important that you have a pull around with an opponent (preferably lots of different opponents) to get used to balance and grip and entries for the throws; the more time you are on the mat the better.

Chapter Two
Taiotoshi (Body Drop)

The following techniques in this book teach you how to take the throw from a static position, which is fine when you are learning the rudiments, but not so good when it comes to dealing with an opponent who is moving around and being awkward. I will not pretend that illustrations in a book can even begin to show movement, but it is enough to say that, once the rudiments of any throw are mastered they should be practised in a randori (free-fighting) situation so that you can throw an opponent who is on the move.

Once you can execute the throw from a standing position, moving uchi-komi (technique work) is highly encouraged. This can be done in lines, so that you move forward and back practising the technique, then uchi-komi in combinations and on the move. So basically you would move around the mat with an opponent and execute five different techniques.

Ippon Shionagi (Shoulder Throw)

You can then include 60 per cent randori (which always seems to end up as 100 per cent randori), then increase to all out fighting. It is imperative though that you get in some sparring work if you ever want to make it work for real. Static work is only useful in the early stages of learning.

After executing a throw on an opponent you have the choice as to whether you want to keep hold of the opponent and finish with ne-waza (ground work) or whether you wish to let him go and either finish with your feet or run away; the choice is entirely yours and is usually determined by the severity of the situation. Some opponents, in their fear, will hold on to you for dear life and you will be forced over with them, taking the fight to the ground.

The body drop is a devastating throw that, when employed properly, puts an opponent out of the game rather clinically, especially with a skilled thrower using perfect entry and timing, and a snap at the end of the throw. It can be executed with or without the appendage of an opponent's clothing.

Judo

Break the opponent's balance to the right front corner. Advance your right foot to the opponent's right foot. Position your body so that your right foot blocks the opponent's right ankle whilst bending your left leg. Because you have broken the opponent's balance by pushing him back he will automatically try to re-establish his balance by coming forward. This is the exact time to catch the energy and take the throw, forward and over the back of your right ankle. This needs to be done with speed and force. As the opponent trips over the back of your ankle, straighten the right leg and drive the opponent forward by pulling with your left grip and driving with your right grip.

Ippon Shionagi (Shoulder Throw)

Judo

Ippon Shionagi (Shoulder Throw)

Judo

To throw without the use of a jacket the same movements are required, only you should wrap your right arm around the opponent's head before executing the footwork.

Chapter Three
Ippon Shionagi (Shoulder Throw)

This is a great technique, it's the one that they always seem to demonstrate (badly) in the James Bond movies where the 9-stone young woman throws the huge baddie clean over her shoulder. Of course it is not as simple as that, but it is a good technique if you can perfect it. From my experience of judo this is the one favoured by most, particularly the variation of the drop shionagi where the thrower drops to his knees to execute the throw. I have to say that this is not my own personal favourite, I am not keen on turning my back completely on an opponent, but I do have many friends that employ it with great success.

Break the opponent's balance backwards, he will automatically push back to realign his balance. As he does so steal the energy given and advance your right foot towards his right foot. Make a body turn, bending your knees so that you are under his centre of gravity. Simultaneously, thrust

Judo

your right arm under his right armpit. Grip hold of his attire if there is any to grab. Keep both of your feet inside of his feet, as shown, and throw the opponent.

Ippon Shionagi (Shoulder Throw)

Judo

Ippon Shionagi (Shoulder Throw)

If you were doing drop shionagi you would drop to your knees, throw the opponent over your right shoulder and slam him into the floor.

Judo

Again this needs to be mastered at a static level and then practised with a moving opponent, progressing to a randori situation. If there is no randori in your practise then you are unlikely to ever develop anything other that a good compliant throw (no matter what your instructor might tell you). In other words it won't work on anyone that doesn't want it to work. The reason I say this is because I am aware that there are systems of grappling out there that do not do any kind of randori. This is daft, you need pressure (and plenty of it) if you want to use this stuff in a real fight. It is very important at this stage that we all know where we stand in regard to methods of practise; if there is no adversity in your training there is no advance. Taking the randori out of your training is like taking the sting out of the bee. Throwing a compliant opponent is completely different to throwing a non-compliant one, the technique is completely different. The confidence and self-esteem that are associated with good grappling systems come from the hard randori, not from a compliant opponent who lets you throw him around all day long. Commercially a system without fighting is great because there

Ippon Shionagi (Shoulder Throw)

is no real threat or danger and so the numbers attending are always high. Practically though it is disastrous because you are not preparing people properly for what is fast becoming a highly violent society.

A shoulder throw is also a good technique to employ when grabbed from behind, but you do have to be very quick because people that grab you from the back usually do it so that they can drag you to the floor and kick your head in before stealing your money (or worse). They don't grab you and just hold you there.

Chapter Four
Ogoshi (Hip Throw)

The hip throw is not really a devastating throw and although it is taught on the curriculum in judo you very rarely see anyone actually execute it under pressure. The reason I have included it in here is because, at a higher level, you can execute advanced versions of the throw that are effective, so it is important to get the rudiments now.

From the conventional lapel or sleeve grip this throw can be both simple and effective though, as with all throws, it relies on a fast explosive entry.

Break the opponent's balance backwards and to the right corner. When he pushes back to realign his balance steal the energy. Simultaneously advance your right foot forward towards your opponent's right foot, feed your right arm around his waist (or head or armpit) and make a body turning in entry and bend at the knees so that your bottom is pushing into his lower abdomen. Make sure that both of your feet are inside the opponent's feet. Throw the opponent forward by straightening your legs and exploding him over your hip. Slam him into the floor. This throw works equally well with or without the added leverage of an opponent's clothing.

Judo

Ogoshi (Hip Throw)

Judo

Ogoshi (Hip Throw)

As a nightclub doorman I used this throw frequently on violent opponent's who tried to struggle when I was dragging them, via a headlock, out of the club. I always used it from the headlock as opposed to 'arm around the waist.' What I liked about the throw was the fact that it allowed me to throw an opponent over with varying degrees of force. If they were very violent I would throw them heavily so that they could not get back up again. If they were not so dangerous I could just tumble them over and control their fall so that, although they were on their back and under my control, they were not injured.

Chapter 5
Osoto Gari (Major Outside Reap)

Osoto is a scary throw. It is one of those throws that devastate an opponent. I have friends who use this technique in a street situation all the time and have to control the fall of the opponent so as not to seriously injure them. It is easily accessible and highly dangerous. Caution should be a priority if you decide to employ this technique.

One of my students, he shall remain anonymous, used osoto on countless occasions in his duties as a police officer. He had enough control over the throw to be able to take people over and manage their fall so that they were controlled but without major injury. Mostly he would just knock the wind out of them, though he did say that not one of his opponents made it to their feet voluntarily after being caught with this technique.

Osoto Gari (Major Outside Reap)

Again this works best from the conventional lapel or sleeve grip (when you get used to throwing techniques you will be able to throw an opponent from any grip).

Pretend to try and pull the opponent forward, he will resist by pulling back, when he does steal the energy and go with his pull. Break his balance backward to the right corner as you simultaneously advance your left foot forward. Continue to draw the opponent's balance outward as you reap your leg to the back of the opponent's right leg. Keep your toes pointed downwards and reap the back of his calf. Pull down with your left hand and drive hard, to the right, with your right hand. Your opponent's weight will now be on his right leg as you reap it from under him, slamming him on to his back.

Judo

Osoto Gari (Major Outside Reap)

Judo

Osoto Gari (Major Outside Reap)

If you want to make the throw a little more gratuitous release your right hand grip and grab the opponent's throat as you throw, driving him backwards with the reap. Sometimes it is also effective to drive the opponent's head backwards by slamming your right bicep under his nose as you reap.

When you reap with osoto try not to wrap your leg around his, it is more effective if you can keep your leg stiff and literally just reap his leg from under him.

Judo

Osoto Gari (Major Outside Reap)

Chapter Six
Ouchi Gari (Major Inside Reap)

Ouchi is not an easy throw to take someone experienced over with, but when you are fighting against an inexperienced grappler, which street fighters normally always are, you can catch them every time. Ouchi is, predominantly, a close range take-down. The problem with this is the fact that it is very difficult to take the opponent cleanly, you normally always get pulled over with the throw. This in itself is not such a bad thing if you are only fighting against one opponent and you can fight on the floor. But if you are facing more than one opponent you could be in trouble. No matter how much you might be able to devour the other fellow on the floor, it will not help if his mates are kicking your head in the process (remember the four B's – biting, butting, blinding and buddies). But then this is the problem with any situation that finds you on the floor fighting with an aggressive foe. It happens, and if it happens you still have to make the best of a bad situation. If you do find yourself on the floor with several

Ouchi Gari (Major Inside Reap)

opponents around you, try to control the person that you are fighting and use him as a shield, so if his mates are attacking you they are also, inadvertently, attacking him. I have had several friends, fellow doormen and martial artists, stabbed by the girlfriends of the men they were rolling around the floor with. It is not safe so don't court it; if the shit hits the fan and you end up on the floor, get to your feet as soon as possible. If you are only fighting the one fellow and you are competent on the floor, that's fine, take your time and do a good job.

What I tend to do with ouchi gari is pull on the opponent as though I am trying to drag him forward. This will force him to react by pulling back up, when he does I go with the energy and break his balance to the back as I simultaneously reap my right leg through and around the lower portion of his left ankle. Then I lift his leg off the ground with my leg as I drive him back over with my right arm.

Judo

On entry you should feel as though you are chest to chest with the opponent; if it is a street encounter you may even butt him in the face on entry. Try and drive him to the floor and stay standing yourself. If you are forced to go over with him then make sure that, as you land on him, you land heavy and hard. Again if you hit the deck make sure that you secure a strong ne-waza position immediately. There is always a mad scramble as soon as two fighters hit the floor, so make sure that you dominate and take the offensive. Most people that you fight in the street, with few exceptions, will only be good for a few seconds after which they'll be like a sack of shit. For that few seconds though they'll be crazily strong indeed.

Ouchi Gari (Major Inside Reap)

Judo

Ouchi Gari (Major Inside Reap)

Ouchi gari is a reaping action, but if for some reason your reap does not take the opponent's balance you could employ ouchi gaki which is the same technique with a hook instead of a reap. When you make your entry and place your right leg around the back of the opponent's left leg, hook their leg up instead of reaping it. Once hooked drive them over on to their back. If at first they do not go just keep hopping forward until they do.

Chapter Seven
Kouchi Gari (Minor Inside Reap)

Kouchi gari is a minor reaping technique that, on the surface, doesn't look like that much of a technique. But once mastered it is fantastic. It is the main technique I use in my randori. The better judo players use this technique quite often to set up a bigger throw like osoto gari. They use the kouchi as a balance breaker (or even a feint). I use it, especially outside, as a trip to get the opponent off his feet and on to the ground, where I can either run away, finish with kicking techniques or follow down to use my ne-waza. If the timing is correct this can be a devastating technique.

This technique can be used at range or very close up. The simplest way is at close range so I'll stick to that for the purpose of this book. The long-range kouchi is a more advanced technique that can be learned as an extension of the smaller version.

Kouchi Gari (Minor Inside Reap)

I like to work this from a strong high right hand grip. I pull the opponent forward and down. This does two things; it brings his right leg forward (if it wasn't already forward) and it forces him to try and pull back up again. When he does I will resist initially to make him think that I am trying to pull him over, then I will suddenly relax and let him pull back up. As he pulls I will steal the energy that this creates and drive him backwards with my strong right arm. Simultaneously I will hook my right foot around the back of the opponent's right ankle and sweep it away as I push, slamming him on to his back.

Judo

Kouchi Gari (Minor Inside Reap)

A more advanced version of this is to time your foot-sweep with his right foot stepping forward. As he transfers his weight from left leg to right, sweep it away.

Judo

Kouchi gari is a sweeping action, but if your sweep does not take the opponent's balance you could employ kouchi gaki, which is the same technique with a hook instead of a reap. When you make your entry and place your right foot at the back of the opponent's right foot, hook their leg up instead of reaping it. Once hooked drive them over on to their back. Again, if at first they do not go over just keep hopping forward until they do.

Kouchi Gari (Minor Inside Reap)

Chapter Eight
Harai Goshi (Sweeping Hip Throw)

This is a variation on the basic hip throw. It is a lot more practical than ogoshi because it employs the strong right leg in a sweeping action (or left if working the opposite way). It is especially effective for close range vertical grappling.

You can't always choose your grip in a real encounter but I do prefer to work this technique from a high right-handed grip. But you could throw the opponent from almost any grip once the technique has been mastered. Also, if you are a good grip fighter you can change one grip for another almost at will. Good grip fighters, like the lads I trained with at the Neil Adams Centre, are brilliant at grip work and no matter how strong a hold you seem to get on them they take it right off again. With some of their snapping grip releases they have actually been known to break the fingers of their opponents (accidentally of course). Again, this is slightly peripheral to this book and should be seen as a separate study. Suffice to

Harai Goshi (Sweeping Hip Throw)

say that I have mentioned it here in the hope that you might explore it more.

As I said, I like to work this from close range with a high right grip. Pull the opponent down with your right hand (if you want him to step forward to expose his right leg also pull him forward so that he steps with the said leg). He will react by pulling back up again, as he does, steal the energy created and quickly advance your right foot towards the opponent's right foot. Then make a turn in entry so that your left foot is positioned next to your right, with knees bent and your bottom driving into his lower abdomen. Pick the opponent up on your hip as you would with a normal hip throw, and then, almost at the same time, sweep the back of your right thigh against the front of the opponent's right thigh. Continue sweeping backwards with your leg and drive the opponent directly forward and over the thigh, slamming him into the floor.

Judo

Harai Goshi (Sweeping Hip Throw)

Harai Goshi (Sweeping Hip Throw)

This is a big throw if you can bring all of the elements together all at once. If you listen to the opponent's energy and go with it, he will throw himself. Sometimes the opponent will create all the energy you need for the throw by the way he moves; if this is the case then all you have to do is reap that energy and throw him over. However, if he is stiff arming you and there is a deadlock in the action it is down to you to create a window of opportunity by moving him around and creating an opening. This though will take experience and a lot of mat work so the more partner work you can get in the better.

Chapter Nine
Uchimata (Inner Thigh Throw)

I have to say that this is a highly skilled throw, much favoured by the international judo set that use it frequently. In normal randori, only the special players seem to be able to pull it off, not so much because it is a highly skilled throw, rather because it is a throw that seems easy to defend once you have a bit of knowledge. So on the mat it will take time to make this throw your own; in the street however we are dealing with unskilled fighters whose only attributes are aggression and strength and even this is limited to how long their stamina lasts. Because of this you'd probably have more joy in a street situation than in the dojo where skilled players use skilled defence. One of the things that I like about this technique is the fact that it can also be used as an attack to the groin. In the dojo, players often whack the thigh into the opponent's groin on the pretext of attempting uchimata in order to slow an aggressive player down a little. It does the job let me tell you. So, if needs be, it can be used as a strike to weaken a strong street opponent.

The entry is very similar to that of harai goshi but the sweeping leg is positioned between the opponent's legs as opposed to on the outside.

Lead with your right leg on this one and work from a high right grip. Pull down on the opponent so that he is forced to pull back up again; when he does, steal the energy this creates to make your entry. Spin and place your left foot as deep between the opponent's legs as possible. Bend at the knees so that you are below his centre of gravity and pick him up on you hip like you would in an ogoshi attack. Almost simultaneously straighten your legs and sweep your right thigh upward and between the opponent's legs whilst pulling him to the front with your grip. Drive him hard into the mat.

Uchimata (Inner Thigh Throw)

Uchimata (Inner Thigh Throw)

There is a lot of commitment with this attack and quite often the thrower goes over with the opponent. As we said earlier, this can be a good thing and it can be a bad thing, depending upon the circumstances. On the mat it is no great shakes either way, but in a street scenario, going over with the opponent could prove fatal.

The entry to this technique is the hardest thing to master, so a lot time should be spent mastering this element of the throw. Isolate the entry if needs be so that you can get in as quickly and cleanly as possible.

Judo

Chapter Ten
Hiza Garuma (Knee Wheel)

This is another one of those little techniques that I find very effective in a real situation. It's so effective because it is so simple. You literally trip the opponent over. It's not the biggest throw in the book, though you can throw a fellow with force, but it does get him over which is the main aim of any throw. As with most of the throws, the hands play a vital role here. When I throw with hiza garuma (or sasi surikomi ashi which is more or less the same throw, but propping the opponent's ankle as opposed to his knee) I use my hands, certainly my right hand, in a punching action, as if I am trying to punch the opponent in the head. My left support arm is used in a strong pulling action.

The control with this throw is excellent, and gives very little opportunity for the opponent to pull you over with him when he goes. Remember that these throws can all be reversed and should all be practised from both sides.

Hiza Garuma (Knee Wheel)

From a right hand grip, step to the right of the opponent (this adds momentum to the pull or push of the throw) as you simultaneously prop the sole of your left foot on the opponent's knee, thrusting your right hand in the direction of his ear and pulling down hard with your left hand. The hand action is often referred to as turning a steering wheel because that is what it looks like. As you pull and push, the opponent will be forced to step forward to stop himself from overbalancing. Because you have propped his leg at the knee he will not be able to step forward and will be thrown over your left leg. Slam him into the floor.

Judo

Hiza Garuma (Knee Wheel)

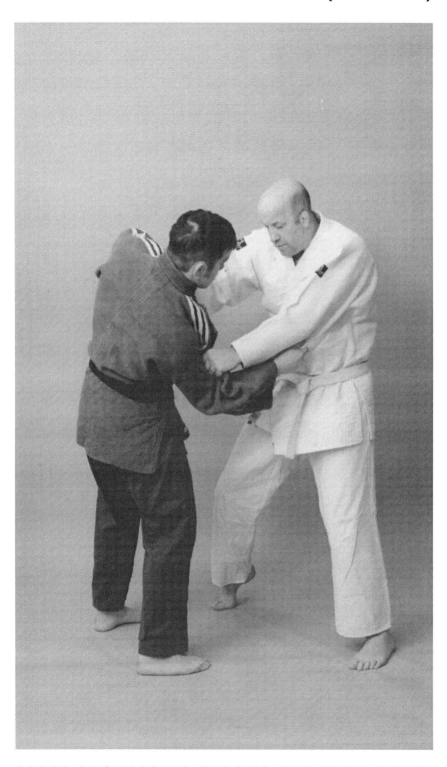

Judo

Hiza Garuma (Knee Wheel)

From here you are in an ideal position either to take the

opponent for an arm bar, release him so that you can finish

from a vertical position, or run away – your choice.

Conclusion

As you can see, all the moves I have included in this text are the main judo throws that differ from the other throwing systems. There are a myriad more throws in the judo system; throws that should be explored in depth if your aim is to develop a good tachi waza (throwing technique). I've tried to be as honest as I can and not just fill your head with a million techniques. I'd rather show you the ones that are most prolifically used in randori and on the street. If you can master these then you'll be ready to try other throws. It's better to be really good at one or two throws that to know a hundred or more but not be able to use them. All the great throwers I have worked with base their whole tachi waza experience around one or two favoured throws. Some use only one throw. They make that one technique so good that it rarely fails.

Please remember that a chain is only as strong as its weakest link and, as far as street defence goes, throwing on its own is not enough. You need to be proficient in all ranges of physical combat from kicking and punching to vertical grappling and ground fighting – all with and without jackets. Many fighters are great at throwing and ne-waza when they have a jacket to use as an appendage, but without it they are lost. Similarly non-jacketed wrestlers rarely know how to take advantage of an opponent's clothing in a real fight. So hit every avenue and leave no stone unturned.

With a contemporary enemy, the main fighting range is that of the 3-second fighter where a physical attack is preceded by some kind of aggressive or even disarming dialogue. In 3-second fighting the punching range is king and all other ranges – as a rule of thumb – are relegated to the realms of support system. Learn to use your hands both defensively and as a strong, clinical attacking tool and most situations will be over before they even begin. If you misread the signs and a fight goes from punching range to vertical grappling then the techniques in this book, and any others that you can use from other throwing systems, will be invaluable.

Judo

Don't forget though that many fighters will not go over without a fight, they will grip and grab hold of you and pull you to the floor with them. If at this stage of the altercation you do not know how to fight on the floor you are already on your way to possible defeat, especially if you are fighting a road digger with forearms like Popeye.

In this text I have shown the throwing techniques in their raw form. Once you perfect them it is wise to practise using the forgotten about 'blow before throw' of old judo. That is, whack them with a strike to set up the energy for a throw. It makes sense. And it's a hell of a lot easier.

As a final point I feel it is my duty to say that I believe violence is not the answer and that we should avoid conflict whenever we can. Long-term, and non-violent, solutions to the problems that we are experiencing in the world should be sought and if you can find an alternative to the violent response I believe that you should use it. Always walk away when the situation allows it, even if that means eating a little humble pie. Ultimately judo, or any fighting art worth its salt, should teach you to walk away with confidence.

Good luck with your practise and thank you for reading my book.

God bless.

Geoff Thompson 2001

The Throws and Take-Downs of Sombo

ALSO IN THIS SERIES:

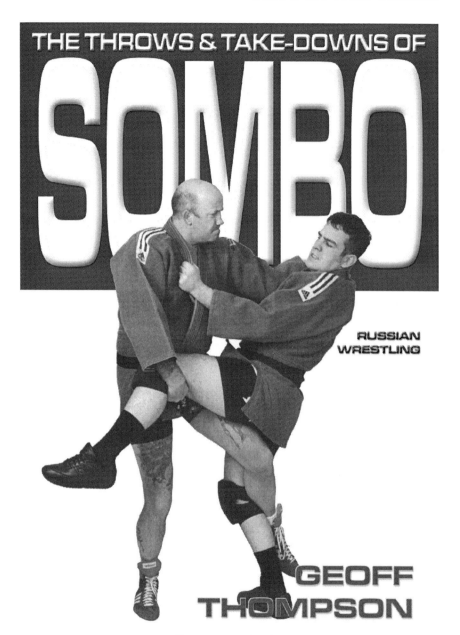

THE THROWS & TAKE-DOWNS OF
SOMBO

RUSSIAN
WRESTLING

GEOFF
THOMPSON

SUMMERSDALE

The Throws and Take-Downs of Greco-Roman Wrestling

ALSO IN THIS SERIES:

THE THROWS & TAKE-DOWNS OF

GRECO-ROMAN WRESTLING

GEOFF THOMPSON

SUMMERSDALE

*The Throws and Take-Downs of
Freestyle Wrestling*

ALSO IN THIS SERIES:

THE THROWS & TAKE-DOWNS OF
FREESTYLE WRESTLING

GEOFF THOMPSON

SUMMERSDALE

Geoff Thompson's autobiography,
Watch My Back

GEOFF THOMPSON

WATCH MY BACK

'I train for the first shot
– it's all I need.'

'LENNIE MCLEAN HAD THE BRAWN, DAVE COURTNEY HAD THE
CHARM, BUT GEOFF THOMPSON IS IN A CLASS OF HIS OWN.' FHM

www.geoffthompson.com

www.summersdale.com